j921
YOU   Westman, Paul.

       Andrew Young,
       champion of the
       poor

DATE			

Andrew Young

Champion of the Poor

by Paul Westman

DILLON PRESS, INC. MINNEAPOLIS, MINNESOTA

Library of Congress Cataloging in Publication Data

Westman, Paul.
    Andrew Young, champion of the poor.

    (Taking part)
    SUMMARY: Profiles the life of the black leader who stood in the forefront of the major civil and human rights movements of our time, served as the ambassador to the United Nations in the Carter administration, and who now serves as the mayor of Atlanta.
1. Young, Andrew, 1932-   — Juvenile literature.
2. Afro-Americans — Civil rights — Juvenile literature.
3. Legislators—United States—Biography—Juvenile literature.
4. Ambassadors—United States—Biography—Juvenile literature. 5. United States. Congress. House—Biography—Juvenile literature. 6. United Church of Christ—United States—Clergy—Biography—Juvenile literature.
[1. Young, Andrew, 1932-   . 2. Afro-Americans—Biography 3. Civil rights.
4. Legislators. 5. Ambassadors] I. Title.
E840.8.Y64W47   1983   973.92'092'4 [B] [92]   82-25106

ISBN 0-87518-239-9

Dillon Press, Inc., 500 South Third Street
Minneapolis, Minnesota 55415

Printed in the United States of America

    2   3   4   5   6   7   8   9   10   91   90   89   88   87   86   85   84

The photographs are reproduced through the courtesy of Operation PUSH, the Religious News Service, Elaine Tomlin, photographer, Mrs. Jean Young, and Mrs. Andrew Young, Sr.

ANDREW YOUNG

For the past twenty-five years, Andrew Young has been in the forefront of the major civil and human rights movements of our time. Except for Martin Luther King, Jr., no other black leader has received as much praise and respect from black people and from whites. Working with Dr. King in the Southern Christian Leadership Conference, Andrew Young helped millions of blacks in the South win their civil rights through nonviolent action. He trained many of the black leaders who were elected later to public office. And perhaps most important of all, he played a crucial role in writing the Civil Rights Act of 1964 and the Voting Rights Act of 1965.

In 1972 Andrew Young became the first black from Georgia elected to Congress in more than a hundred years. He championed the rights of the poor and the powerless who had little power or influence in Washington, D.C. Young was such an effective lawmaker that he gained the respect of leaders of both parties. After he played a key role in Jimmy Carter's 1976 campaign for the presidency, Carter appointed him to serve as U.S. ambassador to the United Nations. Later Young came back to Georgia, where he is now the mayor of Atlanta.

Andrew Young played an important part in many peaceful civil rights protests.

More than a thousand children gathered on a spring morning in 1963 at the Sixteenth Street Baptist Church in Birmingham, Alabama. Almost all the children were black, and some of them were no more than seven or eight years old. They had come to march through the city to show everyone that black people wanted the same rights as whites. Newspeople called them "the children's crusade."

Suddenly police and fire fighters surrounded the children in the church. Eugene "Bull" Connor, the Birmingham sheriff, was determined to keep them from marching. When the young people tried to leave the church, he ordered his men to turn their fire hoses on them. Helpless before the powerful streams of water, the children were knocked down on sidewalks and pushed back against fences. Then the sheriff ordered his men to let loose their dogs to attack the screaming and crying youngsters. Snarling and snapping, the dogs dragged the children along the ground.

TV cameras were there to record the terrible sight. That night people all over the United States and around the world saw what had happened to the black children of Birmingham. They were shocked, and many white people in Birmingham were shocked, too.

Business leaders of the city met with Andrew Young, the black leader who had planned the peaceful civil rights protests. Three days later, black and white leaders announced that they had reached an agreement. All public places in Birmingham would now be open to blacks and whites. Blacks would also have a chance to hold jobs that had been held before by whites only. And all those who had been arrested during the protests would be freed.

Andrew Young played an important part in many peaceful protests like the one in Birmingham. He was one of the main leaders in the civil rights movement of the 1960s. In fact, he helped write the Civil Rights Act of 1964 and the Voting Rights Act of 1965. These laws gave black people rights that they had been denied for hundreds of years. For the first time blacks were able to take their rightful place as full citizens of the United States.

Andrew Jackson Young, Jr., was born in New Orleans on March 12, 1932. Andy's mother, Daisy, was a schoolteacher. She was lively and cheerful, and Andy liked being with her.

Mrs. Young remembers that Andy was a very smart youngster. When he was two years old,

(Left) *Andrew as a baby.* (Right) *Three-year-old Andrew tries out his skills as the neighborhood cowboy.*

he started saying, "I want to go to school." By the time he was three, he was in kindergarten, and at age six he was in third grade. By then, says his mother, he often read comic books to his little brother, Walter.

Andy's father, Andrew Jackson Young, Sr., was a dentist. Mr. Young had a saying for every time his son did something wrong. When Andy lost his temper, his father would say, "Don't get mad, get smart." Andy wasn't always sure what his father meant, but he did know that his father wanted him to learn how to take care of himself. And that wasn't always easy for a young black growing up in a neighborhood of mostly white people.

Andy and Walter usually got along well with their white playmates. They played and laughed with the Irish and Italian kids who lived on Cleveland Street. They went to their white friends' homes, and their friends came over to play with them.

Mr. Young knew, though, that sometimes white kids would say nasty things about his

Andrew (left) *and Walter* (right) *stop for a moment during a game of cowboys and Indians.*

sons because of their color. He told Andy and Walter that they would have to fight these boys to show that they weren't afraid. To help them, Mr. Young set up a boxing ring in the back yard. He hired Eddie Brown, a professional boxer, to teach the boys how to fight.

One day a new boy showed up in the neighborhood. He was much bigger than Andy, and he liked to brag. The new boy decided to pick a fight with Andy. He did not know that Andy was an expert boxer.

The boy stared at Andy. "Hey, nigger," he said.

Andy turned around angrily to face him. "What did you say?"

"I just called you nigger, that's all," the boy replied.

Before he could finish, Andy was on top of him. He punched hard and fast, just as Eddie Brown had taught him. But the new boy was strong, and the fight lasted a long time.

At last Andy won. He learned an important lesson from that fight—talking to people about a problem was better than fighting them. For proof, Andy had only to touch his puffed-up eye.

Andy was lucky that his hardest battles were with the neighborhood bully. For he grew up during the hard times of the Great Depression. Millions of people had lost their jobs, their savings, and in some cases, their homes. The Youngs did not suffer as much as many other families. Both Mr. and Mrs. Young were able to keep their jobs, and they made sure that their children received the best possible schooling.

Even though the Youngs were better off than most people, they could not do many things because they were black. At this time in the South, black people were segregated, or kept apart, from white people in many ways. In New Orleans the Youngs could not eat in white restaurants or use white restrooms. They were not allowed to use the white city parks or the white libraries. When they took a city bus, they had to sit in the back in the section marked for "Colored Only." And even though Andy and Walter lived in a white neighborhood, they went to a school just for black children.

In New Orleans blacks went to their own churches, too. The Youngs, who were a religious family, attended Central Congregational Church. Mr. Young sang in the church choir, and Mrs. Young was the superintendent of the Sunday School. "We always had a rule in our house that if you didn't go to church Sunday morning you didn't go to the movies Sunday afternoon," says Mrs. Young. As a result, Andy and Walter won awards for perfect attendance records.

Mrs. Young believes that her sons learned more about religion from their grandmother than from church. She often asked Andy and Walter to visit their grandmother, who was blind during the last years of her life. When they arrived, she would ask them to read the Bible to her to keep her company. Andy read the Bible so much that he learned it by heart. Years later, he still remembered his grandmother's

Six-year-old Andrew (left), *his mother* (center), *and four-year-old Walter* (right).

favorite saying, "God's gonna take care of you."

Andy learned a lot from his grandmother about caring for people and understanding their needs. His mother remembers that he wanted to help other people, too. He would say such things as, "Let's go see Miss Pierce and talk to her. She's so old and lonely."

One place where Andy did not learn much

was in school. He enjoyed reading, and he read many books about the subjects that interested him. But for Andy, most school subjects were boring. At Gilbert Academy, a private high school, he did only enough work to get passing grades. He tried hard to make sports teams, but he was younger than the other students and was not big enough to play on the school teams.

As a high school student, Andrew sits for a family portrait.

When Andy finished high school, he wanted to go to college in Iowa. However, he was just 15 years old, much younger than most college students. His parents asked him to start at Dillard University in New Orleans so that he could live at home. After one year at Dillard, Andy transferred to Howard University, an all-black school in Washington, D.C. This was the first time Andy had lived away from home.

Since Mr. Young wanted Andy to become a doctor or dentist, he took classes that would prepare him for medical and dental school. Still, he did not like to study as much as he liked sports. By now Andy was taller and heavier, big enough to play on college teams. At Howard he was a star on the swimming and track teams. He also enjoyed going to parties with his friends, especially his steady girl friend.

And yet, Andy wasn't happy because he didn't want to be a dentist or a doctor. In fact, he

Andrew at the time of his graduation from Howard University.

wasn't sure what he wanted to do when he finished his studies at Howard. By the time he graduated, he was a troubled young man who was searching for some purpose in his life.

Andy's parents had driven up to Washington, D.C., to pick up their son and take him home for the summer. On the way back they stopped at a religious camp in King's Mountain, North Carolina. Andy stayed in a room there with a young white minister who was about to go to Africa as a missionary.

Andy admired the minister for wanting to go to a faraway land to work with black people. And in a way, the young man made him ashamed of his own values. "In all my growing up, through college, nobody ever said to me, 'You've got a responsibility to do something for somebody else,' " Andy remembers. "And I thought to myself, 'Now here's a young white guy going off to Africa to work with my people. This is something I should be doing.' "

Andy asked his parents if he could stay on at the camp a few more days. He wanted to find out more about this strange young man who was so different from the whites he had known before. Mr. and Mrs. Young agreed, and Andy got to know the young man better. "He was very thoughtful after that," remembers Mrs. Young.

"And when we got home he said, 'Mother, I gave my suit to that fellow because he didn't have one.' "

In New Orleans Andy met the Reverend Nicholas Hood, a young black minister. Reverend Hood, the new pastor at the Youngs' church, was staying for a short time at their home. Hood asked Andy to travel with him to a religious camp in Brownsville, Texas. Andy decided to go, and he liked the people at the camp so much that he stayed for the whole summer.

The white people in Brownsville reminded Andy of the minister he had met in North Carolina. They weren't going to Africa, but they had big plans of their own. In the coming year, they wanted to win a million young people for Christ. And they asked Andy if he would serve as one of the volunteers in their religious campaign. He would be working for six months, without pay, in the service of the Lord. Andy thought about it, and he said yes.

After a training course in Indiana, Andy was sent to work in Connecticut and Rhode Island. He lived at the Hartford Seminary in Hartford, Connecticut. A seminary is a school where students are trained for the ministry. Andy enjoyed his work so much that he decided to stay right there at the seminary. He called his parents to tell them that he had decided to become a minister.

For the first time, Andy felt that he really had something to live for. Now his life had a sense of purpose and direction. And unlike his earlier schooling, he was eager to study for his classes and to read the books for them.

Andy read about the great religious leaders of history. He especially liked the writings of a leader named Mohandas Gandhi.

Gandhi had led the people of India in their struggle for independence from Great Britain.

He taught them to protest peacefully against unfair British laws. No matter what British soldiers did to Gandhi's followers, they did not fight back. Finally, after 17 years of peaceful protests, the British could stand no more. They gave India its independence.

Andy believed that blacks in America needed a leader like Gandhi. Maybe then, he thought, black people could win some of the rights that white people had denied them for so long. As Andy continued to study and learn, he came to share Gandhi's strong belief in the power of peaceful weapons for change.

Each summer the students at Hartford Seminary put aside their books and did the work of the church. One summer Andy served as the pastor of a church in Marion, Alabama. During his stay there he lived with a number of families that belonged to the church. The first one was the Childs.

The Childs had four daughters. When Andy arrived in Marion, Jean, the youngest, was away visiting her brother in a nearby town. Even though Jean wasn't there, Andy decided that he would like her. He could tell from the things in her room—a Bible, many books, and a Senior Life Saver Certificate—that she shared many of his interests. When Jean came home, he knew at once that he had been right about her. "I decided the Lord had sent me to Marion to get a wife!" he says.

Jean liked Andy right away, too. "I thought he looked like a clean-cut young man—with very large ears!" she remembers. "We were immediately attracted to each other and we worked very closely that summer and a romance grew out of that."

By the end of the summer, Andy and Jean were in love. Andy went back to Hartford Seminary, and Jean continued her education studies at Manchester College in Indiana. They wrote to each other and visited on holidays. On June 7, 1954, just after Jean's graduation, Andrew Young and Jean Childs were married.

That summer Andrew served as the pastor for two small churches in Thomasville and Beachton, Georgia. Afterward he and Jean returned to Hartford Seminary for his last term there. In February 1955, he graduated from the

At Hartford Seminary, Andrew Young is ordained as a minister.

seminary and returned to the two Georgia churches.

Most of the people in Thomasville and Beachton were black, poor, and young. Many of the grown-ups had gone to the North to find jobs. Usually they left their children with grandparents in the South. Andrew and Jean tried to do things with the young people that they could not do without their parents.

Andrew remembers that "...the kids needed someone to work with them. So we cleared playgrounds and built basketball courts and I took them to conferences and to colleges and did for the entire community the things that my parents had done for me."

Nothing that Andrew and Jean did could change the rundown homes and tattered clothes of the black people in this part of Georgia. To bring about real changes, Andrew believed, blacks would have to use their right to vote. That way they could elect new public officials who cared about their needs.

Getting blacks to vote in the South wasn't easy. Most blacks in Thomasville and Beachton had never voted and believed that voting did no good. Even if they wanted to vote, whites found ways to stop them.

One way was to charge a "poll tax" that had to be paid before a person could vote. Most southern blacks were so poor that they could not afford to pay the tax. Another way was to require that all voters pass a written test. Since many blacks could not read, they could not pass this test. When these ways failed, whites threatened to harm blacks or to take away their jobs. Two black ministers in Mississippi had been killed when they tried to get blacks to vote. No one had been arrested for the murders.

A group of whites called the Ku Klux Klan used terror to make sure that blacks stayed second-class citizens. Klan members wore white robes and pointed hoods. When they wanted to scare black people, they burned crosses in their yards. Since they often traveled at night, they were known as "night riders."

The Klan didn't like Andrew and Jean Young because they were encouraging black people to vote. Klan members tried to threaten the young minister and his wife by staging a march near their home. Andrew and Jean, however, didn't scare easily. They went right on helping blacks to vote.

Another young minister who was working to help southern blacks gain their rights was Martin Luther King, Jr. In Montgomery, Alabama, he led peaceful protests against a city law that kept blacks and whites apart on buses. Like Andrew Young, he believed in the teachings of Mohandas Gandhi.

Martin Luther King worked to change the

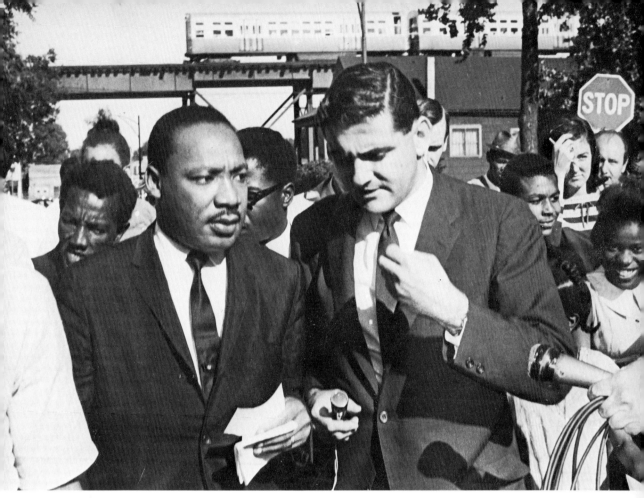

Martin Luther King rallied many black people to join with him in the early civil rights protests.

unfair Montgomery law by leading a boycott against the city buses. The boycott meant that no blacks would ride the buses until the law was changed. Even though they were attacked by the Ku Klux Klan, Montgomery's blacks refused to give in. Finally, after a year of protests, the

U.S. Supreme Court ruled that the unfair city law had to be changed.

Andrew Young was impressed by the courage of Martin Luther King and the black people of Montgomery. Soon he found out that he had a great deal in common with the young black minister. Coretta Scott, King's wife, came from Marion, Alabama, and was a close friend of one of Jean Young's older sisters. Since Jean knew Coretta, she and Andrew stopped during a trip to visit the Kings. Andrew got to know Martin and volunteered to join forces with him in the civil rights struggle.

Andrew, however, was soon offered a job far-away from the South. The National Council of Churches asked him to work in its New York City headquarters. He would be in charge of the programs for young people and blacks. After much thought and prayer, Andrew accepted the offer. Late in 1957, he, Jean, and their two small daughters, Andrea and Lisa, moved to the borough of Queens in New York City.

Life in the big city was a far cry from Thomasville and Beachton, Georgia. As usual, Andrew brought many new ideas to his work. He led youth groups on visits to the United Nations headquarters in New York. There officials from many countries met to discuss world events and problems. Andrew also took youth groups on trips to Washington, D.C., to learn about the workings of government. And he reached many young people by hosting a Sunday morning TV program called "Look Up and Live."

While they lived in New York, Andrew and Jean kept in touch with the civil rights movement in the South. They watched on TV as young black college students staged "sit-ins" at lunch counters in ten states. And they saw what happened to the "Freedom Riders" in the

Blacks in Greensboro, North Carolina, march to show their support for the "sit-ins" at lunch counters throughout the South.

bus station at Montgomery. These brave young blacks were beaten by a mob of whites with ax handles and chains. All the blacks wanted was to have the right to eat in the bus station dining room.

Watching the Freedom Riders in the comfort of their Queens home, Andrew and Jean asked each other, "Why are we here? What are we doing up here?" Then they said what they both felt, "Let's go back south. That's where we belong."

Late in 1961, the Youngs did move back to the South, to Atlanta, Georgia. Andrew was named head of a program to register black people to vote. Working for the United Church of Christ, his job was to make sure that blacks had the proper voting skills and knowledge. Sometimes that meant that Andrew's workers taught people how to spell and how city government worked.

Andrew was also working with other civil rights leaders. In 1957 Martin Luther King and other black ministers had formed a group called the Southern Christian Leadership Conference (SCLC). This religious group worked for equal rights for blacks in the South. It also worked to get the U.S. government to pass civil rights laws that would help blacks in their struggle. Soon after moving to Atlanta, Andrew joined the SCLC.

Before long Andrew's ideas and skills made him an important SCLC leader. In 1964 he was named executive director. Andrew was most valuable to the SCLC as a planner and as a peacemaker who could bring blacks and whites together. He planned many of the civil rights marches and protests of the early 1960s.

In some places, like the city of Birmingham, angry whites attacked blacks in an effort to stop them. Four little black girls were killed by a bomb during a Bible class at Birmingham's Sixteenth Street Baptist Church. Jimmie Lee Jackson was killed by state troopers in Marion, Alabama, during a civil rights march. He was trying to help his mother, who had been beaten by the troopers. In Saint Augustine, Florida,

Despite the danger from angry whites, Andrew Young planned many civil rights protests. Here he attends one in Jackson, Mississippi.

Andrew himself was beaten to the ground by an angry white man swinging a blackjack. Luckily, he was not hurt badly.

One of the most dangerous places for the civil rights workers was Selma, Alabama. There Martin Luther King led hundreds of schoolchildren in a march to the courthouse. All the marchers were arrested and put in jail. After three more days of marches, three thousand people were crowded into Selma's jails. Even the jails in nearby towns were full.

Still, the civil rights workers kept on marching. Sheriff Jim Clark and his deputies surrounded a large group of black children in downtown Selma. Using police cars and trucks, Clark and his men herded the children like cattle. Prodding the youngsters and forcing them to run, the police officers drove them out of town.

People all over the United States were

shocked by what was happening in Selma. Soon hundreds of whites from the North came there to join the black civil rights workers. A march was planned from Selma to the state capitol in Montgomery. On March 7, 1965, the marchers started to cross the bridge that led out of Selma toward Montgomery. As they walked, they sang a freedom song that began, "We shall overcome."

At the other side of the bridge, a line of about two hundred state troopers on horseback waited. When the marchers approached, the troopers told them, "This is an unlawful march." The troopers gave the marchers three minutes to go back to Selma. Instead of leaving, the marchers knelt down on the bridge.

Then, after three minutes had passed, the troopers attacked with tear gas and clubs. Many of the gasping and bleeding marchers fled back across the bridge. Angered by the

*Andrew Young and Martin Luther King lead
the march from Selma to Montgomery.*

sight of the injured marchers, some blacks in Selma went to get their guns.

Andrew Young ran from one apartment building to another, shouting at people to put away their guns. "Get back into the house with this weapon," he yelled. "We're not going to have any weapons out." At last the people calmed down, and the state troopers went away. Like the followers of Gandhi, the civil rights marchers were using peaceful protests to change unfair laws.

Finally President Lyndon Johnson sent U.S. troops to Alabama to protect the civil rights marchers. Andrew Young helped reach an agreement with white leaders. Three hundred people were allowed to take part in the march. They were protected by hundreds of army troops along the route from Selma to Montgomery.

When they arrived at the state capitol,

Everywhere he went, Andrew Young worked hard to make sure that civil rights protests were kept peaceful.

25,000 people were there to greet them. Their leaders were even allowed to meet with Alabama governor George Wallace. He was a white leader who thought blacks should not have the same rights as whites.

The events in Selma convinced President Johnson that a new civil rights voting law was needed. Earlier Andrew Young had helped write the bill that became the Civil Rights Act of 1964. That law was a major step forward for equal rights for blacks in America. Andrew had also played a big role in writing a bill that would help blacks vote. Then he had sent it to President Johnson so that the president could look it over. The president presented it to Congress, and it became the Voting Rights Act of 1965. This law opened the way for millions of blacks from the South to vote in the elections that followed.

Andrew Young wanted the blacks voting for

the first time to believe that their votes really made a difference. If black people could vote for other blacks, he thought, they would be more likely to vote. Andrew started training programs for black leaders who wanted to run for public office. In all, he trained more than six hundred people. Many of them later became sheriffs and mayors of towns in the South.

Andrew Young, Martin Luther King, and the SCLC had brought about some important changes for blacks in the South. They also staged peaceful protests in the North because blacks were treated unfairly there, too. In the North most blacks held low-paying jobs and had to live in rundown buildings in the poorest parts of town.

To help northern blacks, the SCLC sent another civil rights bill to President Johnson. He sent it to Congress, and it became the Civil Rights Act of 1967. This law had a special "open housing" section that said black people had the right to live where they wanted.

In the North and the South, the civil rights workers won battles for black rights. Some whites were angered by the changes because they thought that blacks should remain second-class citizens. A few of these people were so angry that they threatened to kill the SCLC leaders.

Martin Luther King and Andrew Young had received many threats over the years. They had both been beaten, and Dr. King's home had been bombed. Once King had received a threat in Jackson, Mississippi. He and Andrew were about to leave Jackson to drive to Natchez.

Soon they were far out in the country where the road was dark and empty. A car appeared ahead in the glare of their headlights. Suddenly it slowed down, blocking the road ahead. Andrew was driving, and he decided not

Martin Luther King, Jr., with Andrew Young.

to take any chances with the strangers in the suspicious car. Stepping on the gas, he and Dr. King shot past the other car at 90 miles per hour. Andrew did not slow down until the strange car had been left far behind.

Through all the dangers, Andrew remained

cheerful. He remembered what his grand-mother had said to him many years before. And in dangerous places like Birmingham and Selma, he would pass on her faith, and his, to anyone who would listen. "The Lord will take care of us," he would say.

Andrew's faith was tested by the events of April 4, 1968. The SCLC leaders were in Memphis, Tennessee, to help striking garbage workers. Most of the workers were poor and black, and they worked long hours for little pay. Compared to white workers, they were often treated unfairly. Once they were paid for only two hours of work on a day when whites received full pay. The SCLC decided to support the black workers' demand for fair pay by planning peaceful marches in the city.

Martin Luther King announced that he would lead a march through downtown Memphis. Many whites in the city didn't think that the march was a good idea. The Ku Klux Klan warned that it would stage a march to protest against the SCLC march. Meanwhile, some blacks wanted to attack the whites. They marched through the streets waving sticks and holding "Black Power" signs. There was a danger that blacks and whites would start fighting each other.

Dr. King was troubled by the threats made by whites and blacks in Memphis. He could not sleep, and he often stayed up all night talking to Andrew Young and other SCLC leaders.

One evening King went out onto the balcony of the Lorraine Motel where he was staying. From inside the motel room, Andrew heard a sudden shotgun blast. He ran out onto the balcony and found his close friend lying still in a pool of blood.

Andrew shouted for someone to call an

Martin Luther King stands with other SCLC leaders on the balcony of the Lorraine Motel in Memphis. Later he was killed by a shotgun blast while standing here.

ambulance. Dr. King was rushed to the hospital, but nothing could save him. Within minutes he was dead. Sadly, Andrew called Coretta Scott King in Atlanta to tell her what had happened and to ask her to catch the next plane for Memphis. Later, the police arrested a white man named James Earl Ray and charged him with King's murder.

Five years earlier, Martin Luther King had given a speech that many people remembered at the time of his death. He had spoken on the steps of the Lincoln Memorial in Washington, D.C., during the March on Washington. Andrew Young had been in charge of planning the march in which 200,000 people, black and white, came to show they believed in civil rights for all Americans.

Dr. King began the speech by saying, "I have a dream." His dream was that one day blacks would be treated fairly and justly as true Americans. He went on to say, "I have been to the mountaintop. I have seen the Promised Land. I may not get there with you. But I know we as a people will get there." Martin Luther King did not get to the "Promised Land." But by the end of his speech, many of those in the huge crowd had come to share his dream.

Andrew Young was one of the people in the

Andrew Young, Coretta Scott King, and former vice-president Walter Mondale join together to carry on the work of Martin Luther King.

crowd who believed in King's dream. When Dr. King died, Andrew felt that he and other black leaders should keep trying to make that dream come true. He knew, though, that an important part of the civil rights movement had died along with King. Black leaders would have to find new ways to carry on his work.

For a while Andrew continued his work

with the SCLC. Early in 1970, John Lewis, another civil rights leader, asked him to run for Congress. The district Lewis wanted him to run in was made up of Atlanta and some nearby towns.

Andrew believed that he could serve the people of Atlanta well. He knew, though, that no black had been elected to Congress from the South in nearly a hundred years. Even though the odds were against him, he decided to run.

Many civil rights workers, black and white, volunteered to help Andrew Young in his campaign. His volunteers went from door to door all over the district to tell the voters about Andrew's record. Part of the district was in the city, and part was in the country. Black people and white people, rich people and poor people lived there. Andrew tried to let them know that he would serve them all in Washington, D.C. He worked hard to win the campaign.

Flanked by Julian Bond, a black leader,
Andrew Young announces his first campaign
to become Atlanta's representative in Congress.

But when the votes were counted on election day, Andrew had lost. Still, he didn't give up or lose faith in people. In fact, he decided to run for Congress again.

In his second campaign, Andrew visited

every area in his district. He spoke at church meetings, in the homes of rich business people, and in the poorest neighborhoods of Atlanta. This time, when the votes were counted, he had won. He was the first black person elected to Congress from Georgia since 1871.

At his victory party on the night of his election to Congress, Andrew is kissed by his wife Jean (left) *and his mother Daisy* (right).

In Congress Andrew Young was known as a champion of the poor. He wrote bills that helped poor people go to good schools, find well-paying jobs, and receive needed health care. When others in Congress tried to cut programs that helped the poor, Andrew spoke out against them.

Andrew, however, had come to Washington to serve all the people in his district. He worked hard to stay in touch with the voters there. Every weekend he visited his office in Atlanta.

Andrew left his door open so that anyone who wanted to talk with him could come right in. Many people did. Poor people without much money asked him how they could pay their rent. Others asked him to explain difficult government rules they did not understand. Rich or poor, young or old, black or white, he did his best to help them all.

Andrew won the respect of the voters in his district and the members of Congress. In 1974 and 1976, he was reelected to serve new terms by landslide votes. In Congress he was known as a peacemaker who could bring together people whose ideas were far apart. The floor of Congress was usually noisy, even when members were speaking. But when Andrew Young rose to speak, the people on the floor grew silent.

Andrew enjoyed serving the people of Atlanta in Congress, and he would have been happy to stay there. But the 1976 campaign for president of the United States brought about some big changes in his life. It all started with a man named Jimmy Carter.

Carter had been elected governor of Georgia the year Andrew Young first ran for Congress. Andrew was impressed by his record as governor. Carter believed in equal rights for black people, and he had named blacks to serve in his state government. In 1974 he had asked Andrew to give his advice and ideas for Carter's campaign for president.

Andrew Young thought that Jimmy Carter would make a good president. He spoke out for him to groups of blacks and working people all over the country. And he headed a drive that registered 3 million new voters by election day in 1976. When Carter won the election, he owed a big thank you to Andrew Young.

President Carter chose Andrew to attend a meeting of American and African leaders in Lesotho, Africa. When Andrew returned, Carter asked him to become the next U.S. ambassador to the United Nations (UN). The UN was formed in 1945, just after World War II. Almost all the countries of the world are members. Their ambassadors in the UN try to work together to solve problems in peaceful ways.

*Andrew Young, his son "Bo," and former
president Carter gather at a news conference
to announce Andrew's appointment as the
next U.S. ambassador to the United Nations.*

The job of UN ambassador was a very difficult one. Though many of Andrew's friends
advised him not to take it, he accepted the post.
He believed that he could help the United States
get along better with the other nations of the
world. On January 31, 1977, Andrew Young
became the first black ever to serve as the U.S.
ambassador to the UN.

In June the rest of the Young family arrived in New York City to join Andrew. The UN ambassador lived in the Waldorf Towers, a large building with fancy rooms like a hotel. At first Andrew, Jean, and their two youngest children—Paula and Andrew, Jr., or "Bo"—lived there. Andrea, their oldest daughter, joined them when she decided to go to Columbia Law School in New York.

The Youngs wondered how a five-year-old son, a teenage and a college-age daughter, and Snuffy, their dog, would get along in the Waldorf Towers. But the staff was friendly and helpful, and soon even little Bo was at home there.

Andrew made changes in the way that the home and the office of the UN ambassador were run. The ambassador had cooks, servants, and a limousine. Andy, however, did not put on airs. He introduced the butler to visitors, ate

Andrew Young and his family: (from the left)
Andrea, Lisa, Jean Young, Andrew III ("Bo"),
and Paula.

breakfast with his chauffeur, and traded in his Cadillac for a Ford. In his UN office, he hired blacks, women, and Hispanics. He put black art on the walls in place of old pictures.

Unlike earlier UN ambassadors, Andrew Young thought that the United States should listen closely to the views of all UN members. He believed that it should be more friendly and understanding toward the poorer and less powerful nations of the world. Most of these countries are in Africa, Asia, and Latin America. Together they make up more than half the members of the UN.

Large, strong countries often used smaller, weak ones to serve their own needs. Andrew Young believed that using power in this way was wrong. All nations should work together, he said, because each one depended on others in important ways. If the nations of the UN joined forces to work for common goals, the world would be a safer and a happier place for everyone.

Andrew worked closely with the other UN ambassadors to help solve world problems. First he let them know what the United States wanted to do about a particular problem. Then he asked them for their opinions and listened carefully to what they had to say. When votes were taken, the other countries understood why the United States voted for or against something. In this way Andrew gained the trust of the ambassadors of many nations.

The African countries were especially important to Andrew. For hundreds of years, blacks had been brought from Africa to America as slaves. The slaves were freed after the American Civil War. But they did not win their full rights as U.S. citizens until the civil rights movement of the 1950s and 1960s.

For a long time the black people of Africa

were ruled by whites, too, from countries in Europe. Then most African blacks won their freedom at about the same time that American blacks won their rights. In 1977, though, the nations of South Africa and Rhodesia were still ruled by whites. Most of their people were black. The blacks were kept apart from the whites, who had all the power. This practice, called *apartheid*, had not changed in many years.

In the UN Andrew Young spoke out against apartheid. On trips to Africa, he worked to help end apartheid in South Africa and Rhodesia. While he was there, he made important friends for the United States among the leaders of black African nations. He said that in the past many white nations had treated black people unfairly. And he urged all black people to stand up for their human rights.

President Carter supported Andrew Young's views on apartheid and human rights. He

On a trip to Africa, Andrew Young greets a black leader in Tanzania.

thought that Andrew was doing a fine job of making friends for the United States around the world. "Andy Young is a good ambassador," Carter said. "He is open, skillful, and honest."

Some of the things Andrew said, however, embarrassed the president. Because Andrew was so honest and open, newspeople found that his comments made headlines. Often they took just a little part of what he said and twisted it around so that it became a big story. Newspaper and magazine writers attacked him for talking about some unpleasant truths. Before long, some U.S. government officials began to say that he was too outspoken for his job at the UN.

Finally, after two and a half years at the UN, Andrew Young decided that it was time for him to leave. "I'm not sorry for anything I've said or done," said Andrew. But he knew he could not continue as UN ambassador without the full support of highly placed U.S. government leaders. By the fall of 1979, he no longer had that support.

Andrew returned to his home in Atlanta for

a well-deserved break from public service. Before long, though, he was running for the office of mayor of Atlanta. "I decided I'm a public person," he said, "and there's nothing more exciting than America's cities. That's where the challenge is." In November 1981, he won the election to become Atlanta's next mayor.

As mayor, Andrew Young believes that he is carrying on the struggle that began with the civil rights movement. The challenge today, he says, is to make sure that poor people have the education and skills needed to find good jobs. Since one out of four Atlantans is poor, the challenge is great.

Yet even during the hard times, Andrew has kept his faith in himself and in his work. "Wherever I am, I've got to do whatever it is I feel needs to be done at that moment, and I have to do it well," he says. "I can't worry about whether my future is endangered because of what I'm doing. I have to do simply what I think is best at that moment."

Throughout his life—as a young minister, civil rights leader, Congressman, UN ambassador, and mayor—Andrew Young has shown that faith, courage, and hard work can change our world for the better. The people who have known him have high praise for his work. President Carter said of him, "Of all the people I have known in public service, Andrew Young is the best." A well-known black minister calls him "the voice of black people in this country."

Whatever the future holds for Andrew, one thing is clear. He will continue to speak out for the right of all people to be treated with fairness and justice. For his strong faith in God calls him to serve as a champion of the poor in this world.

The Author

Paul Westman is a regular contributor to *Current Biography* and has written many books for young people, including several for the Taking Part series. Of the series, Westman says, "Young readers will learn something about well-known contemporary men and women in many challenging fields and at the same time begin to discover some of the joys of reading."

A recent graduate of the University of Minnesota, Westman lives in Minneapolis.